The Last Train from Paris

and other stories

of the Holocaust

Mireille Taub

Lamberson Corona Press

West Babylon, NY

2025

Dedicated to the six million Jews who perished in the Holocaust. (1933-1945)

I am one of the lucky who survived, but many of my extended family were among the victims. Their memory and their stories live on in these pages thanks to my surviving family who carried these accounts across the ocean. These are but a few stories. A tiny fraction of the lost testimonies of the millions who have no one to recognize their lives or tell their truths.

We always remember them.

We shall never forget.

Mireille Taub

To the Forces of Evil: The joke is on you ...

Table of Contents

Introduction

How do we define courage? We can use examples that fall under the headings of determination, purpose, sacrifice, tenacity, endurance, and resistance. We see all of this in war,.but war brings out the beast in us as well as the best in us. We will not honor the beast, but rather, dwell on the best, the courage it takes to deal with excruciatingly difficult circumstances, the courage to find ways to survive, the courage to promote positive change and help others.

This book tells of the time Jews were targeted under the Nazi occupation and the courageous people of my family who tried to defend the values of the French Republic; those of Liberty, Equality and Brotherhood.

LAST TRAIN FROM PARIS:

Escape and Refuge, 1940

In September 1939, while my parents were on vacation in Fontainebleau with extended family members, Hitler invaded Poland. This act of aggression invoked mutual aid pacts and Europe was finally at war. My extended family immediately returned to Paris and volunteered to serve France. With the advent of hostilities, my father immediately petitioned the American Consulate for evacuation and began to prepare an escape route via Bordeaux to Spain. In fact, he traveled to Bordeaux hoping to be able to send for us or send us along during the beginning stages of the "phony war." Paris was under constant bombardment alert and, although not many bombs had actually fallen, the terrified citizenry , sought nightly refuge in makeshift bomb shelters built under apartment building cellars and in the Metro.

Gas masks, resurrected from the First World War, and re-issued, were constant companions. Ration tickets for supplies such as food, coal, and clothing were issued to prevent stockpiling, looting and black marketeering.

For several months, the war in France was called the "phony war" with few military advances, but in the spring of

1940, the war exploded in full military action, with France quickly losing. In the last days of French fighting, my father was at last mobilized and told to report to a command post in Paris. He came, equipped with his visas, and exit papers, requesting permission not to serve because he felt, not only did he risk being killed in what was now viewed as a totally futile war, but, because of imminent surrender putting his wife and family at extreme risk. In his case, compassion won and my father was released from his French Army commitment and told to get back to his family.

Meanwhile, my mother packed a small suitcase with just enough clothing for several changes and waited for my father to return. My family managed to get to the railroad station and we were able to take the last train from Paris just hours before Paris surrendered to the Nazi forces. Our train came under attack. Frightened refugees hid in the bushes, expecting to be hit by strafing fighter bombers intent on killing the civilian population, but we survived and joined the long march of refugees, all walking in search of safety in any of the small French communities. We walked, walked, and walked. When we were tired, we walked slower, but we continued walking, away from the war zone. My father and mother took turns carrying me. Even today, my French shoes, attest to the number of miles we covered in our search for safety.

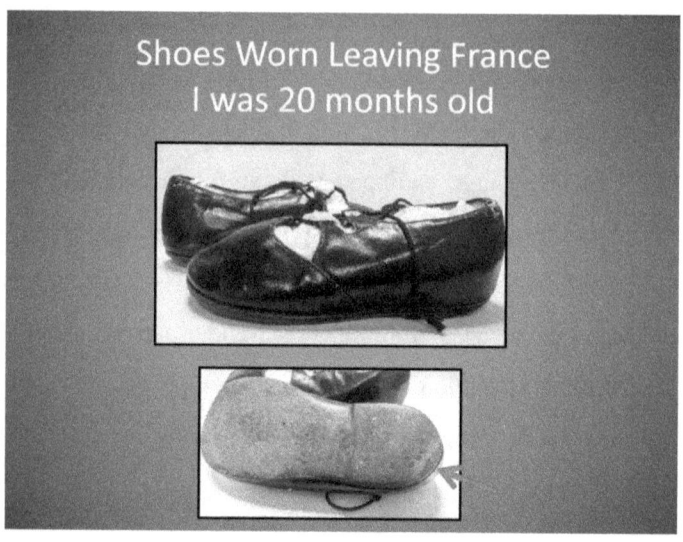

The shoes I wore while walking to safety after our train was bombed. Note the worn-out sole and heel.

My father tried to get us to Bordeaux, as per our original plan, but the area was proclaimed a "forbidden" area because of its strategic position not far from the Atlantic Ocean. A recently found document showed that we stayed in a town named Monitory from June 28 th to July 8, 1940, during which time my father tried to find a way into Spain.

Through another of life's quirky moments, while waiting on line, in Monitory as Bordeaux was totally inaccessible, perhaps to re-validate a document or receive information about other travel possibilities, my father met the American consulate officer who had helped him in Paris. She needed to get to Marseilles where the American Government was setting up the consulate serving Vichy France. She spoke a little French and could drive. My father, fluent in French and local dialects couldn't drive, but had a couple hundred American dollars. So they pooled their resources, rented a truck, and drove across the Pyrenees towards the Mediterranean. She was protected by her American status as a Consulate Officer; my father provided the language, know-how and some ready cash to buy gasoline, supplies, etc. Together, they headed for the Pyrenees and the Mediterranean coastline, traveling across France to Spain to Portugal, June and July, 1940.

I am not sure why they chose to drive across France, rather than cross into Spain through the Pyrenees at any point during the route. Perhaps they didn't and couldn't trust the fascist Spanish government. In addition, crossing the Pyrenees, under the best of conditions was extraordinarily difficult. In peacetime, guides were there to help. During the war, on the other hand, passeurs or smugglers, could be persuaded and bribed to help, but it was virtually impossible to know whom to trust during a war. And so, we continued towards the Mediterranean. Most likely, my parents, thinking along the lines of Plan B, hoped to take a boat from a port city.

After some time, probably two or three weeks or more, we arrived in the small city of Perpignan which is less than 100 kilometers from the Spanish border. My parents caught their collective breaths and took stock of what they had on hand and in the small suitcase they had hastily packed. They looked at my sister and realized that she had outgrown or worn out her shoes and before they could continue, they would have to replace them with new ones that she could wear. They stopped into a shoe store, located on a large plaza. After a few minutes, they realized that I was nowhere to be found. They were in a total panic; hundreds of refugees were milling around in that square and as a not-quite two-year-old toddler, I could have wandered off anywhere. However, within a short period of time, I was located. I had crawled into an empty shoe carton and was found happily playing with all the shoes left in the carton.

We stayed in Perpignan very briefly and found some means of crossing the mountains into Spain. I am not sure how this was done, probably by bus, but I am sure it was extremely dangerous, and my parents knew that, despite their exit visas, they could have been sent back into Occupied France and into prison camps or worse.

When we finally made it to Spain, we traveled by train to Barcelona. We were allowed only to travel through Spain, but not to stay. The newly established leader of Spain, Generalissimo Franco, a devout fascist, was happy to collect a transit tax from refugees, but he didn't want them in his deeply impoverished country. From Barcelona, we traveled to Lisbon, embarking on a Greek merchant freighter that was part of a convoy. We spent three weeks crossing the North Atlantic, trying to avoid German Uboats that were hoping to torpedo ships heading towards America.

We arrived in America on August 11, 1940. My father's journal records a terrible voyage. Boat tickets mention hammock beds, probably a very cramped stateroom. and less than adequate fresh food. Six weeks of travel across war zones in France, Atlantic storms, U-boats, grossly inadequate and horrible food had finally taken their toll on me. Upon our arrival at Ellis Island, immigration doctors told my parents that I was too ill to be taken off the Island. I had a fever, hives and was a very unhappy toddler. My mother successfully convinced them that there was nothing more serious than the accumulated stress of our experience.

While on board the boat, my father sent cables to various family members telling them when we were scheduled to arrive, but when we did disembark at the pier, there was no one there to greet us. No one had received the telegrams. What he had not realized, or was never told, was that security blackout because of U Boats in the shipping lanes inhibited communication. My father hailed a taxi, who in true NY style, instead of taking us directly to HIAS, (Hebrew Immigrant Aid Society) which was a short distance away, took us on the proverbial scenic taxi ride around Manhattan Island, leaving my father with only $10.00. We stayed in the shelter at HIAS for several days. Finally, "cousins" returning from vacation, found the delayed telegrams, and came to rescue us.

My parents decided not to go on to Chicago, as many of their relatives lived in New York. With their help, we rented an apartment in Williamsburg, Brooklyn. One of the "cousins" provided my father with an introduction to a pocketbook manufacturer in Manhattan. My parents enrolled in school to learn English. My father joined the Civil Defense League, doing night-time patrol, warning citizens of air raid alerts and black out regulations. We were on our way to becoming Americans. We were extraordinarily lucky to be able to escape France. I grew up, a happy child in Brooklyn, NY. I knew that there was a war, however my childhood was very different from what my relatives experienced.

Other family members were not lucky. My mother's sister, Luba, and her daughter Lily died in the Warsaw Ghetto. My father's sisters and families were denounced by Polish peasants while they were attempting to hide in a haystack. They were bayoneted by German patrols looking for Jews. The only one in this family group that survived was Genia who was able, because of her non-"Jewish" very Polish looks, to pass as a Pole. She later emigrated to Israel. My mother's sister, Simone Anker, her husband, and her daughter Madeleine were rounded up in Paris on July 16, 1942, and transported east to concentration camps. Madeleine, who was a top ranking student in Paris, died in Auschwitz. Her parents' place of death is unknown. My other French aunts, uncles and their children also did not survive.

In 1942, my father went to Washington for a special hearing in order to try to bring my maternal grandmother, her husband, and my mother's brother, Leon from Vichy France.

My father's sister and her family, Henri, my father's brother-in-law, all had been demobilized after the FrancoGerman Armistice and had been able to rejoin his wife and son, outside of Paris, somewhere in non-occupied France. We later learned that they managed, under harrowing circumstances, to get across France to Marseilles and eventually Algeria. My father was accompanied by his cousin Bernard Chizever who was to serve as an interpreter, appeared at a hearing presided by a judge who quickly realized that my father had a more than adequate knowledge of English. My father was able to convince the judge that these people were not enemy agents or a threat to the US population. My grandparents, uncle's aunt, and cousin sailed from Marseilles to Casablanca. Much to their great astonishment, they were met on the boat that was taking them to New York. Uncle Morris, (married to my mother's older sister, Madeleine) was also demobilized and returned to Paris. They were warned about the mass roundup of Jews by a neighbor, and were able to escape to Limoges with my Aunt Madeleine and Cousin Monique. Uncle Morris was interned there because he was a "foreign national, not a French citizen" who had crossed the border illegally. Madeleine was picked up by the police for questioning, handed her daughter, Monique to a park friend until she hoped she could return. Monique stayed with this person for some time; Madeleine, was eventually released, having been able to prove French identity, and so the family managed to survive, immigrating to the United States in 1947.

When the war ended, my parents had already decided not to return to France. My father started his own business, becoming a well-known, successful handbag manufacturer.

ACTS OF COURAGE: REMEMBERING FIFI

When Jews were targeted under the Nazi occupation, courageous people tried to defend the values of the French Republic; those of Liberty, Equality and Brotherhood. Arthur Koestler said, "Courage is never to let your actions be influenced by your fears." Fifi, a friend of my brother-in-law, embodied this principal. My husband was 8 years old in 1940 when France surrendered to Germany. His brother, Jacques, was 10 years older and fought for France although he was not yet a French citizen. Many of Jacques friends were of similar age, and most, recent immigrants to France. Some were not yet totally fluent in French, were still struggling economically but rushed to defend France in both the regular French Army as well as the French Foreign Legion trying in vain to halt the Nazi invasion. One of Jacques friends, Maurice Fefferman, nicknamed Fifi, was part of a group of young men who organized themselves into one of the first resistance groups in Paris. They called themselves the Army of Shadows. They were socialists, communists, and many were Jewish. They came from Poland, Armenia, Russia and were extra-ordinarily courageous. They worked in pairs, specializing in killing German officers. Obviously, they worked in stealth, in the dark, silently using close contact killing devices such as knives or their bare hands. They were loyal to each other to the point of folly. They made pacts that if any were caught the others would try to defend them. The inevitable happened, Fifi and his partner had killed another Nazi officer and in attempt to escape, Fifi's partner was fatally wounded. Fifi didn't know that and returned to help his friend. He was badly wounded and captured by the Nazis. He was taken to the hospital and tortured in the hope that he would reveal the names of his band of friends. He refused and died of his wounds, His parents were notified, and surprisingly (or maybe not) allowed to reclaim his body for an appropriate Jewish burial to be held at their synagogue which had not yet been closed. (This would happen a bit later.) My father-in-law, longtime friends of the family, attended the funeral in spite of the terrible danger of the possibility of being caught in a round up of those Jews attending the service. Fifi was buried with tradition, as well as honor. He is now remembered with a commemoration plaque in the neighborhood in which he lived. He, and others, are powerful examples of the capacity of resistance, literally "grace under fire" and inspiration to others who continued struggling to survive. The Army of Shadows Organization personified courage. They faced danger and death with bravery and determination. Although they were the victims of the most extreme racism, they would not allow themselves to be defined as victims. The bravest are surely those who have the clearest vision of what is before them, glory and danger alike, and yet go out to meet both head on.

(The Army of Shadows was made into a (French) film in 1969)

Memorial Plaque in Paris

Maurice Fedderman, nicknamed Fifi

Vacation at Fontainebleau, France, Circa 1937

Madeleine Anker, and my older sister, Raymonde Shyko

REMEMBERING MADELEINE

I was too young to remember *La Petite Madeleine*. All I knew was that my cousin was called *La Petite Madeleine* (little Madeleine) because our aunt was also named Madeleine. In trying to imagine what little Madeleine was like, I think of a slender child caught up in circumstances beyond the comprehension of civilized people.

I was one of the lucky ones. My parents and I were able to escape Paris just before the Nazis occupied it during World War II. Madeleine, along with her parents, Simone and Leon Anker as well as other family members, left behind, was unable to leave. They tried to survive in a city occupied by invaders sworn to exterminate any vestiges of European Jews.

Family pictures of Madeleine reveal a dark-haired, somewhat intense gangly pre-adolescent looking back at the world through long lashed eyes. Her face, lit with a shy smile, hints at her intelligence, but does not reveal the number of academic prizes she had won, her charm, her endearing ways, or quick wit. What little I know of Madeleine was I learned from piece-meal comments told reluctantly, in low muted tones of regret, by my mother, her former playmate, David, whom I later married, and my aunt Madeleine.

She was born in Paris, around 1929. Her mother, my Aunt Simone, was born in Poland and had left Warsaw with her family as a young girl. (France was the 2nd country of choice for immigration.) She met her husband, Leon, also a Polish immigrant and was married in Paris. Madeleine's father adored his daughter Madeleine, spending hours with her encouraging her love of literature. They earned a precarious living selling books from a pushcart. Business was not always brisk, and Madeleine's father was often his own best customer.

After 1940, the new German occupation regulations prohibited Jews from maintaining a business unless it had an Aryan manager. This edict forced many Jews to close their small stores. My aunt Simma and her husband, Leon, were no longer able to work. They were obliged to live off whatever savings they had. Like other Jews, they were forced to wear a fragile yellow rayon star of David to indicate their religious affiliation. Obviously, this made them easier targets, as well. Some shops would not sell to Jews. Jewish patients could no longer easily receive medical services. Jews were forbidden the use public transportation, go to movies, libraries, and other public places because of the risk of being caught up in a dragnets triggered by random searches, violation of racial laws, and curfews.

My husband, a bit younger than Madeleine, told me that because Jews were allowed to do so little, much of their free time, if possible, was spent within the family circle sharing food, supplies, and both difficult and joyous moments. Yes, there were those, too; the comforts of family and friends and the blessings of surviving another day. An earlier raid of their apartment had bought them time. Leon, sickly and frail, had lined up all his medications on his night table. When the French police and Gestapo had come for them, Simone claimed her husband had tuberculosis, hence the array of medicine bottles on the table and nightstand. They, fearful of contagion, did not enter the apartment. However, in July 1942, in the largest citywide sweep made by the French police at the request of the German authorities, a roundup of all the foreign-born Jews living in Paris occurred. My cousins' luck had run out. From what we could learn, she and her family were taken to a sports arena (Vel d'Hiver) that served as a holding tank for the captured Jews. They were held there for several days lacking basic sanitation, water, or food. From there, her parents were sent to semifinished army barracks in Drancy, a suburb of Paris. Madeleine was separated from her parents and sent to Beaune La Rolande, an internment camp not far from Orleans. These civilian prisoners, men, women, and children were then crowded into cattle cars and transported to death camps in Poland. I do not know when or where she died.

Several years ago, at Yad Vashem, I was finally able to trace, through extensive cross-referencing, books about children's transport, written by Serge and Beatrice Klarsfeld. Madeleine, separated from her parents, was sent to Beaune La Rolande, transported to Auschwitz, and died there. Her name was recently inscribed at the Shoah Memorial to France's Lost Children dedicated in Paris, March 2005. Little Madeleine will live in our memories as long as her story is told.

Madeleine Anker's name, along with her parents, posted
on Memorial Wall at Shoah Memorial Paris

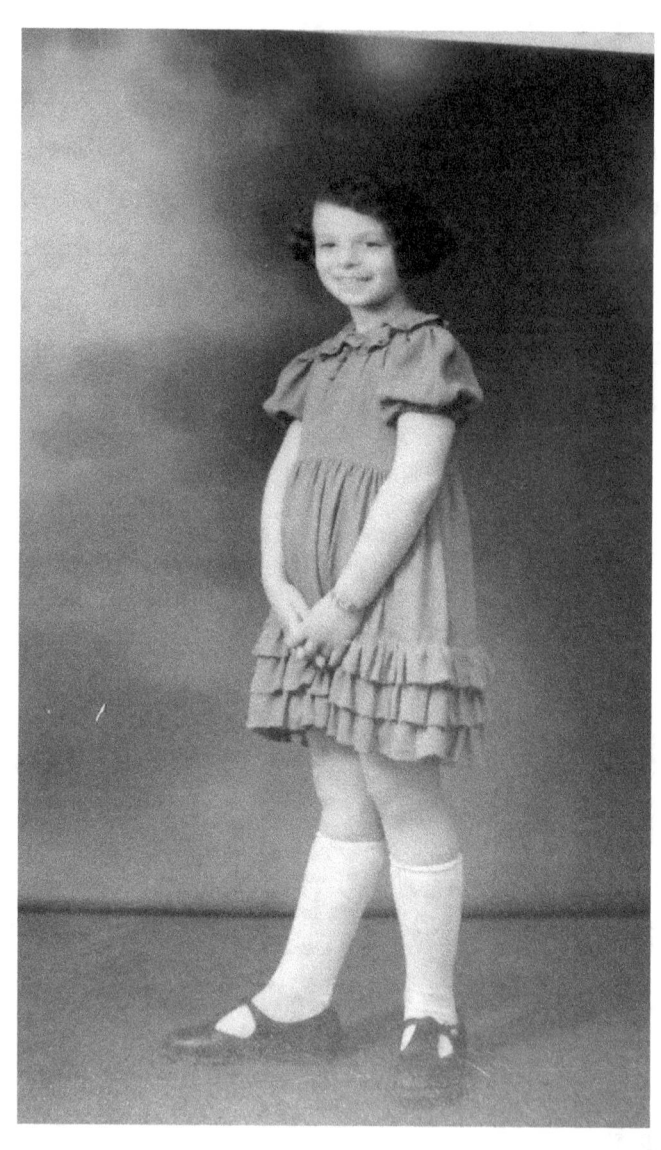

Madeleine Anker, circa 1936

Shoah Memorial in Paris June 2009

Translation: Dedicated to the memory of students from this school, deported from 1942-44 because they were born Jewish, innocent victims of Nazi barbarism and the Vichy Government. More than 300 children from the 9th Arrondisment were exterminated in the death camps. Madeleine was one of them.

PostScript: While speaking to the curator at the Shoah Memorial in Paris, she pulled out a photograph of a family, mother, father, and two older teen age boys. It was a typical "happy family" picture, usually taken to commemorate an important event, but what I found shocking, in looking at this picture, was that they were all wearing identifying Stars of David. How could they be a "happy family?"

Asked if I recognized them, I, regretfully, had to say "no," explaining that I was not quite two when I left Paris. The curator thought they were possibly my family because I mentioned that I found several of my great-aunts and uncles names on the commemorative wall and she thought because of other identifying factors that these photos were members of the same family. As she started to pull them away, I realized that I did, indeed, recognize one of the teenagers. He was my mother's cousin Daniel (her favorite cousin) I had seen his picture many times in my mother's album. I was asked if I was sure, and although I was "reasonably sure" I couldn't be 100% positive. How tragic that these lives, ending in unspeakable horror, cannot even be identified for other generations to remember!

Family Portrait: Summer 1938
Petite Madeleine, Morris Szertag
Gussie Szwertag

Left to right: Madeleine Anker (killed in August 1942)
Madeleine's maternal grandparents, Morris Szwertag,
Gussie Szwertag (escaped to NY, 1942) their daughter
and son-in law (my parents) Estelle Shyko, Sylvain
(Sidney) Szaijko (Shyko) Raymonde Shyko (escaped to
NY, August, 1940)

POR VOUS, MADEMOISELLE;

FOR YOU, MISS

He was tall, handsome, twinkling blue eyes and totally charming. He was my mother's brother, the 2nd oldest sibling, preceded by Luba but followed by three sisters. I suspect that he knew he was charming and would and could probably talk himself out of most of the situations in which he found himself because of his great credibility and aforementioned charm. I remember his telling me bedtime stories about his escapades such as trying to fly off the balcony of his mother's apartment in Warsaw and engaging in activities that most middle-class Jewish boys knew enough to steer away from and not try. To my five-year-old sensibility he sounded as if he could be my contemporary and friend (if my mother allowed me that kind of "dangerous" friendship.) I now wonder whether he really did all the things he spoke about, but I suspect that, yes, some of those adventures were real.

In fact one of his escapades got him into trouble with the police, not a good idea in antisemitic circles of Warsaw and his mother and stepfather sent him away from the family home to school in Danzig. While living there, he acquired another language and was now able to speak

28

fluently in German, Russian, Polish, Esperanto, Yiddish, Hebrew, and some French. He decided to emigrate to France along with his parents and three sisters after the first World War. Luba, newly married, stayed in Warsaw, much to the great regret of her family who were not as enamored of her husband as she was. In France, Leon became a tailor/pattern maker, reinforcing skills he probably learned at his mother's knee. Her family had been engaged in making the costumes for the Jewish National Theater of Warsaw. He was a bachelor during the Jazz Age in Paris, certainly having the time of his life. I heard about his girlfriends (not from him) but from a relative who knew him at the time. His reputation preceded him as I grew in maturity. My father, in the middle of the war (1941-2) had been able, with great difficulty, to obtain a visa for him, his mother, stepfather and 3 other relatives after appearing at a special hearing in Washington DC. He arrived in New York during the summer of 1942. He arrived with new best friends that he made aboard the ship; friends of his who became part of my family life for the rest of their lives.

Let me tell you more about Leon, some of which I found out after he passed away. When my parents were able to get out of Paris on the last train leaving before Paris surrendered to the Nazis, our families were left behind, their much hoped for visas not yet having arrived. My mother asked my uncle to go to our apartment to retrieve important memorabilia such as some treasured wedding gifts, photo albums, etc. (Did I say that Leon was a gifted photographer and many of the mpictures in that album were taken by him when it was not common to be a gifted amateur photographer.) I know from the back-and-forth letters, written in several languages, French, Polish, Yiddish, and even in English to my sister that my mother saved through her long life that Leon tried to mail her the package. (Who knew that Leon arrived in the US with an ability to get by in English?) I am not sure that he was successful in mailing her the package containing her life memories and treasures or that he kept this precious package until he was able to get out of Occupied France to North Africa (Casablanca, Algeria) and then on the Serpo Pinto to NY (Yes, the same ship on which Matisse and others that Varian Fry saved were also able to board.) But let us talk about life in Paris under the heel of the Nazi occupiers. Fraught with ever present, imminent danger, daily survival hung on luck, some planning (if one were lucky) and hope. Some of the conditions that were imposed on the conquered population included the following:

* Severe rationing for the general population but even more so for Jews who were only allowed to shop during very limited, specific hours (often after food supplies had run out)

* Curfew on the general population, more stringent for Jews, not allowed to be out for the same (limited) amount of time that non-Jews were permitted.

* Discrimination in the workplace; Jews were not allowed to work in certain jobs.

* Jewish students were no longer allowed to attend university.

* Registration of Jewish identity at the local police station with that "J" stamped on ID papers.

* The required wearing of a visible label of a Star David identifying the wearer as a Jew, to be targeted whenever, and always the fear of being caught in random

One day, while waiting online in a grocery to request what few rationed needed food could be had, Leon struck up a conversation with the young woman waiting behind him on that same line. He was young, good-looking, and charming and, of course, liked to flirt. When asked by the grocer what he needed, he was given a few of the items on his list and told that this was the last of those items. The young woman with whom he was flirting, sighed, saying something like, "I needed that for my elderly relative" Leon turned to her and probably with a flourish, handed over the requisite items, saying "Pour vous, Mademoiselle" (For you, Miss)

Several days later, Leon was caught in one of those random dragnets and brought to the nearby police station. Much to his astonishment, the secretary handling the procedure of those captured, was the young woman with whom he was flirting. She recognized him, and in some way, managed to convey to him that the people captured were to be put on a truck, train and then east to the prison and death camps. She also (whispered, I am sure) that she was with the resistance and would try to help him. Somehow, she was successful in separating him from the group, and, in some mysterious way, was able to get him out of the police station and back on the street. Again, I don't know how, but at that point in time, Leon was able to cross the demarcation line between Occupied France and Vichy France. The letters that Leon sent to my mother covered some of this time period, but since they were written in French, Polish and Yiddish, I was only able to translate the French. Perhaps the other letters would answer the many questions that I still have. Leon found employment in his trade as a tailor, sometimes moving from one place to another. He managed to contact his mother and stepfather who were also, at this point, in unoccupied France. He even told of correspondence with his sisters who had remained in Paris. One letter mentions the sister who had never left Warsaw who in a letter to one of her "French" sisters describes the conditions in the Warsaw ghetto as very harsh but livable. Then Leon went on to comment that one can never be sure of what the French sister (recipient of the letter) said and meant. His letter to my mother reflected his increasing concern about his safety as well as his parents and questioned why the necessary paperwork for their visas had not progressed more quickly.

The letters stopped in July 1942; I have no idea how he and my grandmother and her husband were able to travel out of France to Casablanca nor how their boat passage was assured. I do know, much to their great surprise, they were also traveling, as mentioned earlier, on the same ship as my father's sister, Jeanette, her husband Henri, and my cousin Marcel. I have to suppose that my father (probably with the help of Cousin Charlie in Chicago) made the financial and physical arrangements. I was four years old when the family arrived, obviously much to everyone's great joy and relief. Leon continued to charm everyone, especially his two nieces. My sister and I loved spending time with him. We never knew what stories he might tell, what games we might play, which people we might meet. He seemed to enjoy his bachelor life but eventually met Sara with whom he fell in love. Unfortunately, Grandma gave him a very hard time, never "cottoning" to Sara who was a blue-eyed redhead nurse originally from Reykjavik, Iceland. Although in truth, she probably didn't want anyone marrying her devoted son, she also was against his marrying anyone who wasn't Jewish, which was the reason he never married the woman he was associated with in France. Grandma didn't believe Sara who claimed that she was Jewish, brought up by her French-Jewish grandmother, originally from Lyons. In fact, Grandma insisted that Sara meet with our rabbi who proceeded to test Sara about her knowledge of Hebrew (which she could read) and her knowledge of Judaism. Sara apparently passed with flying colors and was grudgingly permitted to marry Leon. Leon picked my 12th birthday as his wedding date, a date, he said, jokingly we would always remember. And we did, always calling each other to share good wishes. Leon moved to Baltimore with a better job and away from his mother who was unceasingly hostile towards his wife.

I visited Leon every summer. He always treated me with great respect and consideration considering that I was evolving from a pre-teen to a what I hoped was a sophisticated woman of the world. Every summer we made a pilgrimage to Washington DC, visiting new sites and revisiting favorites. Conversations swirled around current events, past events, literature, music, evolving with the times that were a'changing from the 50's into the volatile 60's. He adored my husband, fondly, remembering him as an alert verbal child from the pre-war days. They too always had intense, meaningful conversations about the vicissitudes and challenges of our new world. Then Leon had a critical incapacitating stroke, but lived several more years because of the devoted nursing care of Sara who couldn't bear putting him in a nursing home. He is buried next to his mother; hopefully not arguing with each other, each at peace. I distinctly imagine his turning to Sara and telling her, "Pour vous, Madame" as he pointed to what would, 20 years later, be her final resting place, in spite of Grandma's resentment.

LOOKING BACK

Today, as I write this on April Fool's Day, 2025, I look back reflecting on a personal cosmic joke. The cosmic joke was played on the forces of evil, rampant fascism that had decreed that my family, my kind were superfluous, evil, and not worth being part of humanity. Not only did I survive, along with my parents and sister, and several close relatives, but I grew up having had a happy childhood, and a satisfying career. I can say, with great pride, that indeed, both professionally and personally I contributed to my world and community.

Even though I grew up in Brooklyn, during WW2, well aware that there was a war out there that impacted on family members, I had the prototypical childhood…school, (loved it) piano lessons, scouts and neighborhood buddies. My parents were my role models for being pro-active and standing up for one's beliefs and the right and "proper" thing to do. I carried their example into high school and college becoming heavily involved with student government and other campus organizations. My first trip back to Paris, junior year, was an academic adventure and pilgrimage. My courses were entirely in French which I understood, of course, but was somewhat less proficient in speaking it as I had refused to speak it as a child preferring my American identity. Art, Architecture, and Literature buzzed through me. I re-connected with those family members who managed to survive, met and married my husband who had spent the war years as a hidden child. He too was one of the lucky ones as were both his parents and his older brother, hiding in different ways and in different places.

My husband immigrated to NY and found employment as an engineer in the burgeoning space/tech industry. The company for whom he worked sent him back to Paris to manage the European office and so, we became hybrid expats; truly Franco American so to speak. We were brought back to the States after more than five years, settling on Long Island where I found my true professional love. I taught in Freeport for 34 years as a literacy specialist and after my retirement, taught at Nassau Community College and worked as an independent consultant for NYSUT doing staff development in school districts in both Nassau and Suffolk counties. I also served as an advisor to NY State Ed for teacher certification and literacy competency tests.

Retired people do keep calendars. I must because after the death of my husband, I became increasingly active at the Nassau County Holocaust Memorial and Tolerance Center, located in Glen Cove, NY. I serve as a docent, survivor speaker, educator and chair the David Taub Reel Upstander Film Series, named after my husband who was an ardent film enthusiast. We are entering our 13th year of alternating films dealing with the Holocaust experience as well as films highlighting targeted populations. In addition to my deep commitment to HMTC, I am secretary of the Long Island Arts Council in Freeport, chairing several of our art initiatives, and belong to two very different writing groups which meets monthly.

And, of course, there's family life…ever present, ever heartwarming. I have 3 children, 3 grandchildren and I am so very proud of them as I see them perpetuating my family tradition of pride, involvement, and civic engagement.

To the Forces of Evil: The joke is on you. My mother frequently, and in at least three languages, quoted the following: "Man proposes, God disposes." My Father said, "Life is for the living (he didn't know the expression "Carpe Diem") along with "Aggravation I don't need." Although life changed irrevocably for my family and me, we were fortunate to survive to lead happy, productive, and meaningful lives.

Historical Documents

1940: Parisians Flee the City as German Troops Advance

BY INTERNATIONAL HERALD TRIBUNE
June 11, 2015 8:22 am
Comment:
*During the German occupation, the Paris Edition ceased
to print and would not reappear till December 1944, after
the liberation of Paris*

*As the German invasion progressed unchecked, the
Parisians began their exodus from the city ahead of the
invading army. The foreign respondent, Walter B. Kerr,
described the atmosphere of the city in the last edition of
the newspaper distributed in Paris on June 11, 1940:*

Paris, before dawn yesterday, was a city of men, women
and children fleeing to safety, of countless thousands of
families joining the millions of refugees from the north who
have fled before the German mechanized army in these last
few weeks.

All day long streams of cars and trucks, loaded down until
the springs gave way, poured out of the city. It was
heartbreaking to watch them for there once more was that
sad old story that has been told so many times, of twisted
lives, of poverty, of flight before an invader, of separation
perhaps forever from mothers and fathers and children.
They lined up at railroad stations, carrying overwhelming
bundles. They piled into old cars that hammered and
pounded their way along the roads.

I do not know exactly when they began to realize their city
and perhaps their lives were i4n danger, when they made
up their minds that they would have to run if they were to
live much longer in a France that was really France and not
French soil occupied by German troops in field-gray.

It must have been some time around 8 or 9 o'clock Sunday night for by 2 and 3 in the morning thousands of homes had been closed and clothing had been piled in the streets. You could see men and women pouring stuff in back seats, on the tops and hoods of their automobiles. And the exodus was under way.

Someone had told a friend and he had told someone else. The news spread fast. By dawn the trucks were pulled up before government offices and heavily laden packing cases were being jammed inside them. Everyone had work to do and everyone was doing it frantically. It was almost impossible to get a taxi. They were pressed into service to move families to the railroad stations. The police stopped cars in the streets and requisitioned them for military and government use. Occasionally, a line of military lorries raced through the city at high speed, or a motorcycle dispatch rider. Many shops closed their doors. Cigarette merchants put all their stocks on display. There would be no need to economize. There was a rush on stores selling bicycles and by 3 p.m. these had nothing to sell but bicycles for children.

Americans joined in the rush, most them business men who had waited until the last minute, wives who had not wanted to leave their husbands, and some newspaper men, following the government. But the American Embassy was open for business and staying open for business. Ambassador William C. Bullitt and most of his staff will be at work at their offices at 2 Avenue Gabriel, no matter what happens.

And of course there are still thousands of Parisians here and some of them were still in their favorite cafés last night, although they looked pretty lonely. They just do not want to leave home, that is all; or they cannot. Tomorrow, they will read their papers as usual, for an order issued early yesterday afternoon was countermanded by Georges

Mandel, the Minister of the Interior, and newspapers may be printed today. They were published yesterday afternoon, although they printed little news, of a Cabinet meeting which was later called off; last-minute military commentaries containing little information that was not in the morning papers; general headquarters morning communiqué, the 561st of the war, and one of the shortest.

There was a story from Rome in each newspaper, two paragraphs long, that the Black Shirts of Rome were to meet a 5 o'clock and that "the general sentiment is that Mussolini will make a great speech on this occasion." It was not until later over the radio that the people heard the real story.

If this story gives a picture of only confusion in Paris, it is an inaccurate picture. There are many calm people here, men and women with great confidence in their army, which is still fighting one of the greatest battles of all time against terrific odds in men and material. —

New York Herald Tribune, European Edition, June 11, 1940

OBRIGADO SENHOR SOUSA MENDES

"I would rather stand with God against man
than with man against God."

This is about a time when all the stops were pulled out, literally and figuratively. This is about a time when the people in this narrative had the courage to do whatever it took.

Setting:

Time: June 1940
Place France: The crowded roads toward Bordeaux leading out of France towards Spain The road through Toulouse and then to the Mediterranean coast

Characters:

Aristide Sousa Mendes, top ranking Portuguese diplomat in France

Sylvain Szajko, Estelle Szajko, and their daughters, Raymonde Szajko (6 years old and Mireille (Mimi) Szajko (20 months)

Thousands of refugees trying to flee France in what was called the exodus; many Jews, heading towards Bordeaux, a strategic Atlantic port city, that was also the seat of the highest Portuguese representative in France; Aristides Sousa Mendes.

During the last week of May 1940, my father told my mother to pack a small suitcase and be ready to leave Paris as quickly as possible. France was losing the war and would, like Holland and Belgium, be quickly overrun by the rapidly advancing Nazi troops. He intended to plead to be excused from his call up before the commanding officer of his future unit where he was to present himself for military service in was to be France's last stand. It took courage to present his reasons for not serving as he felt that as a loyal resident of France, he was very grateful for all the opportunities France had given. However, it was more important for him to save his wife and children who would be in extreme danger should something happen to him. He eloquently stated his reasons starting with his personal status as a Jew, married with young children, along with his permission from the American government to be evacuated, and repatriated; supported by all the proper documentation. Not, he nor my mother, or my sister and I were American nationals. My mother, sister and I were French nationals, my father was considered by the American government to be "stateless" as Poland refused to recognize his Polish birth, in spite of having a Polish birth certificate and for a number of reasons, he was unable to become a French citizen in spite of having lived in France for many years. It took a great deal of personal courage to say that although he loved France, he loved the safety of his family more. In addition, it also took courage as well as empathy from the commanding officer to agree with him and then to dismiss him from his military obligation. My father returned home, gathered up family, critical papers and documents and that small suitcase filled with modest changes of clothing that hopefully would last as long a time as this exodus might take. And, of course, a tin box containing my mother's sewing kit in case repairs were needed.

It took courage to brave the hordes of people crowding the train station, board the overcrowded train that I was later told would be the last train to leave Paris prior to an expected Nazi victory. We were on our way to Bordeaux. Our train was bombed which was a typical cowardly tactic used by the Nazis to terrify the civilian population. It was imperative that we reach Bordeaux to be able to obtain a Portuguese visa that would allow us to leave Europe to arrive at the safety of our ultimate destination. Unfortunately, we were not allowed to enter Bordeaux as the French government closed down the city as they negotiated their surrender. Miracles can occur especially under extraordinary circumstances. That's why these events are called miracles. By happenstance, my father met the American consulate officer who had prepared our exit papers. She immediately recognized my father from having helped him with his unusual papers. (He had been issued a Nansen Passport, only one of 2000, that Thor Nansen, through the League of Nations had created for refugees who were also considered "stateless." She offered us a ride across France with a stopover in Toulouse where Aristides Sousa Mendes had appointed surrogates to approve appropriate visas.

Once in Toulouse, my father was able to contact Aristides Sousa Mendes appointee, actually a Frenchman, who provided us with the necessary visas to be able to enter Portugal. We continued our journey across France to the Mediterranean coast where we were dropped off in Perpignan. From there we crossed the border into Spain. We had to pay the Spanish authorities a transit tax for passing through, but were not allowed to get off the train to stay in Spain. Once more we crossed the border, this time into Portugal where my father was able to obtain passage on a Greek freighter which part of a convoy of ships crossing the Nazi submarine infested waters of the North

Atlantic. I was told that we slept on hammocks, the conditions primitive. I was stopped at Ellis Island because I had broken out in a rash; My mother managed to convince the doctor that the rash was due to stress, trauma, poor conditions, lack of proper food and so we were released.

Years later I learned that Aristides Sousa Mendes was charged with high crimes for disobeying President Salazar's orders not to help Jewish refugees. He was called back to Portugal, tried, and found guilty. At his trial he said, "I would rather stand with God against man than with man against God." Sousa Mendes died in poverty on April 3, 1954 owing money to his lenders and still in disgrace with his government. On 18 October 1966, Yad Vashem recognized Aristides de Sousa Mendes as Righteous Among the Nations. Today, I say with deep respect, "Obrigado Senhor Sousa Mendes." Without your help, I would not be able to share my story.

Aristides de Sousa Mendes

Known for Saving the lives of thousands of refugees seeking to escape the Nazis in WWII.

Visa Recipients:

SZAJKO, Estera née CZERNIEWICZ P A
Age 30
SZAJKO, Mireille P A T
Age 1
SZAJKO, Raymonde P
Age 5
SZAJKO, Szlama P A
Age 31

About the Family:

The SZAJKO family received Portuguese visas in
Toulouse signed by honorary vice-consul Emile Gissot
on July 12, 1940 under the authority of Aristides de
Sousa Mendes.

They crossed into Portugal and sailed to New York on
the vessel Nea Hellas in August of 1940.

Photos

Szlama and Estera Szajko

Raymonde and Mireille Szajko

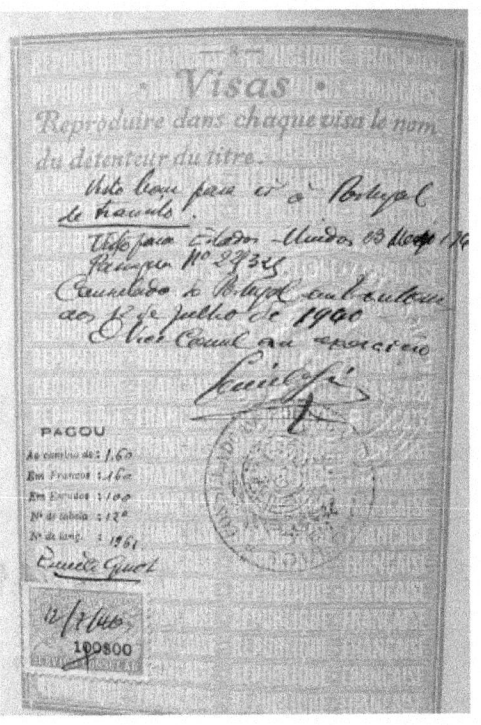

PORTUGUESE VISA ISSUED TO ESTERA SZAJKO IN
TOULOUSE ON JULY 12, 1940 SIGNED BY EMILE
GISSOT UNDER THE AUTHORITY OF ARISTIDES
DE SOUSA MENDES

PORTUGUESE VISA ISSUED TO SZLAMA SZAJKO
IN TOULOUSE ON JULY 12, 1940 SIGNED BY EMILE
GISSOT UNDER THE AUTHORITY OF ARISTIDES
DE SOUSA MENDES

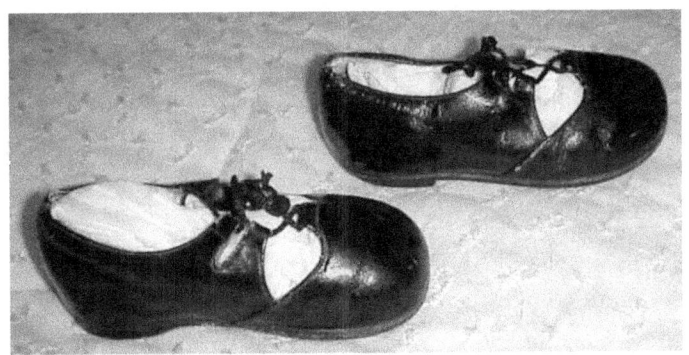

SHOES WORN BY MIREILLE SZAJKO
DURING THE EXODUS

TESTIMONIAL OF MIREILLE TAUB NÉE SZAJKO

I was born in Paris, on October 7, 1938. The world
political situation was rapidly worsening due to the rise of
Nazism in Germany. My maternal grandmother, wise to
the ways of deteriorating social conditions because of her
Polish background, urged my parents to arrange to leave
France should conditions worsen. Both my father and
mother were born in Poland.... One of the major
impediments to obtaining the appropriate visas was the
fact that because my father, having left Poland before the
age of conscription, had never served in the Polish
National Army, he therefore was not recognized by the
post war government as a legal citizen of Poland.... Nansen
passports, named after the Norwegian diplomat who
sponsored these papers, were issued by the League of
Nations to people that were unable to prove a national
identity. Approximately 2000 in total, they were mainly
issued to White Russians, who, after the Russian
Revolution needed to immigrate to safe places. I suppose
that perhaps my father was able to be issued a Nansen
Passport because the village in which my father was born
was on that fluctuating border between Russia and

Poland.Although my sister and I were both born in France, my parents had to petition the French Government for citizenship status, which was granted, but not without filing numerous papers and fees. The years between 1934, my sister's birth and 1938, when I was born were filled with increasingly serious international, political and economic crises. War became inevitable in spite of Chamberlain's optimism. Papers, affidavits, visas were submitted, returned, and recognized. Passport applications were filed, received, and placed within accessible safe keeping....

With the advent of hostilities, my father immediately petitioned the American Consulàte for evacuation and began to prepare an escape route via Bordeaux to Spain. In fact, he traveled to Bordeaux hoping to be able to send for us or send us along during the beginning stages of the phony war. Paris was under constant bombardment alert and although not many bombs had actually fallen, the citizenry, terrified, sought nightly refuge in makeshift bomb shelters built under apartment building cellars and in the Metro. Gas masks, resurrected from the First World War, and some, reissued, were constant companions. Ration tickets for supplies such as food, coal, and clothing were issued to prevent stockpiling, looting and black marketeering....

We stayed in Perpignan very briefly and found some means of crossing the mountains into Spain. I am not sure how this was done, but I am sure it was extremely dangerous and my parents were sure that, despite their exit visas, they could be sent back into Occupied France and into prison camps and worse. Once in Spain, we traveled by train to Barcelona, allowed only to travel through Spain, but not stay in Spain. From Barcelona, we traveled to Lisbon and embarked on a Greek tramp steamer. We spent three weeks crossing the North Atlantic, trying to avoid U-boats, looking to torpedo ships heading towards America. We arrived in America on August 11, 1940. My father's journal records a terrible voyage. Boat tickets show hammock beds, probably a very cramped stateroom and less than adequate fresh food.

Six weeks of travel across war zones in France, Atlantic storms, U-boats, grossly inadequate and horrible food had finally taken their toll on me. Upon our arrival at Ellis Island, immigration doctors told my parents that I was too ill to be taken off the Island. I had a fever, broken out in hives and was a very unhappy toddler. My mother successfully convinced them that there was nothing more serious than the accumulated stress of our experience. We were extraordinarily lucky to be able to escape France. Other family members were not.